Little Book of

FLOWERS

National Library of Australia

Canberra 2002

Published by the National Library of Australia
Canberra ACT 2600
Australia

© National Library of Australia 2002

National Library of Australia Cataloguing-in-Publication entry

Little book of flowers.

ISBN 0 642 10758 0.

1. Australian poetry.   2. Flowers—Poetry.   I. National Library of
Australia.

821.0080364

Compiled by Della Thomas
Edited by Wendy Mehnert
Designed by Kathy Jakupec
Printed by Goanna Print

Front Cover Illustration
Ellis Rowan (1848–1922)
**Phaleria blumii, Bentham,
Modecca australis R.Brown** c.1886
gouache and watercolour on paper; 55 x 38 cm
Pictorial Collection R2170

Back Cover Illustration
Ellis Rowan (1848–1922)
[Ellis Rowan's Garden at Derriweit, Mount Macedon] c.1885
gouache and watercolour on paper; 28.6 x 18.4 cm
Pictorial Collection R9926

CONTENTS

ॐ

From YE WEARIE WAYFARER

Adam Lindsay Gordon (1833–1870)

Hark! the bells on distant cattle
  Waft across the range,
Through the golden-tufted wattle,
  Music low and strange;
Like the marriage peal of fairies
  Comes the tinkling sound,
Or like chimes of sweet St Mary's
  On far English ground.
How my courser champs the snaffle,
  And with nostril spread,
Snorts and scarcely seems to ruffle
  Fern leaves with his tread;
Cool and pleasant on his haunches
  Blows the evening breeze,
Through the overhanging branches
  Of the wattle trees:

Onward! to the Southern Ocean,
  Glides the breath of Spring,
Onward, with a dreamy motion,
  I, too, glide and sing—
Forward! forward! still we wander—
  Tinted hills that lie
In the red horizon yonder—
  Is the goal so nigh?

Extract reproduced from *Poems of Adam Lindsay Gordon*
(Oxford University Press, 1923)

Ellis Rowan (1848–1922)
Queensland Silver Wattle (Acacia podalyriifolia) 1880s
gouache and watercolour on paper; 53.5 x 35.7 cm
Pictorial Collection R2048

WARATAH AND WATTLE

ঽ

Henry Lawson (1867–1922)

Though poor and in trouble I wander alone,
  With a rebel cockade in my hat;
Though friends may desert me, and kindred disown,
  My country will never do that!
You may sing of the Shamrock, the Thistle, the Rose
  Or the three in a bunch, if you will;
But I know of a country that gathered all those,
And I love the great land where the Waratah grows,
  And the Wattle-bough blooms on the hill.

Australia! Australia! so fair to behold—
  While the blue sky is arching above;
The stranger should never have need to be told,
That the Wattle-bloom means that her heart is of gold,
  And the Waratah's red with her love.

Australia! Australia! most beautiful name,
  Most kindly and bountiful land;
I would die every death that might save her from shame,
  If a black cloud should rise on the strand;
But whatever the quarrel, whoever her foes,
  Let them come! Let them come when they will!
Though the struggle be grim, 'tis Australia that knows
That her children shall fight while the Waratah grows,
  And the Wattle blooms out on the hill.

Reproduced from *Poetical Works of Henry Lawson*
(Angus & Robertson, 1925)

Ellis Rowan (1848–1922)
Sydney Wild Flowers 1890s
chromolithograph print; 41.5 x 54.7 cm
Pictorial Collection   U3550

From EVE OF SUNDAY

Ethel Anderson (1883–1958)

'Sarsaparilla false has gone
  Where a naughty flower must go,
To that region now has won
  Clematis' pretended snow;
    'Ring-a-ding' the Bell-birds cry,
    'Ting-ling' Christmas knells reply,
    None is sad but I.

'Prinking out the grass with puce
Trigger-flowers trap flies and beat them,
Art, they say, must come with use,
  You have charms, let truth complete them;
    Are those joys which, honey-sweet,
    So entice my eager feet,
    Tell me, are they, too, a cheat?'

Extract from 'Eve of Sunday' reproduced from
Sunday at Yarralumla: A Symphony
(Angus & Roberston, 1947)

Ellis Rowan (1848–1922)
[Hardenbergia comptoniana] c.1880
gouache and watercolour on paper; 54 x 37.3 cm
Pictorial Collection R2284

Ellis Rowan (1848–1922)
River Red Gum (Eucalyptus camaldulensis) 1880s
gouache and watercolour on paper; 55.7 x 38 cm
Pictorial Collection R2191

SOUTH COUNTRY

ॐ

Kenneth Slessor (1901–1971)

After the whey-faced anonymity
Of river-gums and scribbly-gums and bush,
After the rubbing and the hit of brush,
You come to the South Country

As if the argument of trees were done,
The doubts and quarrelling, the plots and pains,
All ended by these clear and gliding planes
Like an abrupt solution.

And over the flat earth of empty farms
The monstrous continent of air floats back
Coloured with rotting sunlight and the black,
Bruised flesh of thunderstorms:

Air arched, enormous, pounding the bony ridge,
Ditches and hutches, with a drench of light,
So huge, from such infinities of height,
You walk on the sky's beach

While even the dwindled hills are small and bare,
As if, rebellious, buried, pitiful,
Something below pushed up a knob of skull,
Feeling its way to air.

Reproduced from *Kenneth Slessor: Collected Poems*
(Angus & Robertson, 1994)

Ellis Rowan (1848–1922)
[Rock lily (Dendrobium speciosum)] 1887
gouache and watercolour on paper; 54.7 x 38 cm
Pictorial Collection   R2576

From TUMULT OF THE SWANS

Roland Robinson (1912–1992)

The rock-lily's pale spray,
like sunlight, halts my way
up through the unpierced hush
of birdless blue-grey bush.
The rocks crouch on their knees
in earth, torsos of trees
and limb-boughs lead up where
the cliff-face scales the air.
Out from you, rock, my friend,
I lean and, reaching, bend
the scentless pale spray back
to me and see the black
spots in each orchid flower.
O, my love, what power
keeps you curled and bound?
Tormented, the earth's round
begins again. What rock
holds you where you lock
yourself from me? Alone
this spray breaks from the stone.

Extract reproduced from *Tumult of the Swans*
(Edwards & Shaw, 1953)

Ellis Rowan (1848–1922)
[Dampiera linearis, Needhamiella pumilio,
Agrostcrinum scabrum, Hibbertia cunninghamii,
Sphaerolobium] 1880
gouache and watercolour on paper; 54.5 x 37.8 cm
Pictorial Collection R2294

DOMESTIC POEM

Douglas Stewart (1913–1985)

My wife, my life, my almost obligatory love,
Heaven forbid that I should seem your slave,
But perhaps I should say I saw you once in the garden
Rounding your arms to hold a most delicate burden
Of violets and lemons, fruits of the winter earth,
Violets and lemons, and as you came up the path—
Dark hair, blue eyes, some dress that has got me beaten—
Noting no doubt as a painter their colour and shape
And bowing your face to their fragrance, the sweet and the sharp,
You were lit with delight that I have never forgotten.

Reproduced from *Southerly*, No.2, 1983

WONGA VINE

Judith Wright (1915–2000)

Look down; be still.
The sunburst day's on fire,
O twilight bell,
flower of the wonga vine.

I gather you
out of his withering light.
Sleep there, red;
sleep there, yellow and white.

Move as the creek
moves to its hidden pool.
The sun has eyes of fire;
be my white waterfall.

Lie on my eyes like hands,
let no sun shine—
O twilight bell,
flower of the wonga vine.

Reproduced from *A Human Pattern: Selected Poems*
(Angus & Roberston, 1990)

Ellis Rowan (1848–1922)
[Wonga Vine (Pandorea pandorana)] c.1891
gouache and watercolour on paper; 54.6 x 38 cm
Pictorial Collection R2363

ORCHID AND BLACKBOY

David Campbell (1915–1979)

Nodding greenhoods from the stone
Like contemplation grow:
Take care, their thought has broken free
As tigersnake and crow!

Thought set the bud in tea-tree bough,
On her frail eggs the wren.
Who would have thought from chips of stone
With spears would spring up men?

This is the thinking of the rock
That blackboys with their spears
And snake and fledgling celebrate
And orchids at their prayers.

Reproduced from *David Campbell: Collected Poems*
(Angus & Robertson, 1989)

Ellis Rowan (1848–1922)
[Cooktown orchid (Dendrobium bigibbum), Thursday Island] c.1891
gouache and watercolour on paper; 54.7 x 38 cm
Pictorial Collection R2225

From 30 HAIKU

Harold Stewart (1916–1995)

THE NOON CONVOLVULUS
Ah! It will never wash its face of blue
In dew of morning or in evening dew.

—Yayu

AFTER THE HEAT
A moonlit evening: here beside the pool,
Stripped to the waist, a snail enjoys the cool.

—Issa

Extract reproduced from *Australian Poetry in the Twentieth Century*
(William Heinemann Australia, 1991)

Ellis Rowan (1848–1922)
[Convolvulus, Jasminum] 1889
gouache and watercolour on paper; 54 x 37.2 cm
Pictorial Collection R2122

Ellis Rowan (1848–1922)
[Iridaceae] 1880s
gouache and watercolour on paper; 54.7 x 38 cm
Pictorial Collection R2119

From CANTICLE

James McAuley (1917–1976)

Stillness and splendour of the night,
When, after slow moonrise,
Swans beat their wings into the height,
Seeking the brilliant eyes
Of water, where the ponds and lakes
Look upward as the landscape wakes.

The loved one, turning to her lover,
Splendid, awake, and still,
Receives as the wild swans go over
The deep pulse of love's will.
She dies in her delight, and then
Renews her tender love again.

Where fragrant irises disclose
A kingdom to the sense,
The ceremony of pleasure goes
With stately precedence;
Like rich brocade it gleams and glooms
Through the heart's dim presence-rooms.

Extract reproduced from *Collected Poems 1936–1970*
(Angus & Robertson, 1971)

STURT'S DESERT PEA

Swainsona formosa

ॐ

Timoshenko Aslanides (b.1943)

Even driving a car you carry water here
  and think about it, noting presence or absence,
planning every necessary stop around it,
  its promise, threat, its various likely places.
How much more the worry travelling with thirsty horses?
  Still a flower can stop an expedition,
to outback Australia—west of wherever you happen to be,
  east of the west-most reach of the Desert Pea,
a silky, hairy, annual and perhaps perennial forb,
  forever running out on prostrate branches
to show-off long-stalked outward-facing flower-clusters,
  sentinels watching, ancient soldiers defending,
petals shields of red on a blackened central boss—
  and rich and impossible intensity.
Even the ground beneath the flower takes on its hue
  and holds the thirsty men in admiration.
A Latin name is noted in the *Narrative*,
  but this plant's chosen its discoverer.

Reproduced from *AnniVersaries*
(Brandl & Schlesinger, 1998)

Ellis Rowan (1848–1922)
[Swainsona formosa, commonly known as Sturt's desert pea] 1880s
gouache and watercolour on paper; 54.5 x 38 cm
Pictorial Collection R2589

Ellis Rowan (1848–1922)
Cassia laevigata, Queensland c.1891
gouache and watercolour on paper; 53.5 x 37 cm
Pictorial Collection R2412

From PLANTING THE DUNK BOTANIC GARDENS

ॐ

Mark O'Connor (b.1945)

Slowly, between floods and strikes, stuff came.
 Twice a cyclone passed that could have blown
my shrublets all away: the tides by luck stayed low.

 First came creepers for the walls and trunks;
a smother of scented beauty: gay allamandas,
 scented rangoon creeper, jasmines,
convolvulus, tecomanthe, bougainvilleas,
 petrea's lilac statement, climbing cactus (night-
blooming, scented, large), jade-vine, clitoria (a perfect
 replica of the thing in china-blue), great granadillo
the melon-passionfruit on trellis-breaking vines—
 a crop to lure me back—then bamboo liana
that ties whole groves together, the fish-tail
 palm, caladiums, watery aglaonemas,
plus *Cassia fistula* the weeping golden-shower
 that brings giant bumble-bees, bananas,
birdsnest-ferns, dracaenas, umbrella-tree the strangler
 whose crimson spikes drip a daily gallon
of nectar for birds, bats, bees to quarrel over,
 plus native tree-ferns. I turned that dusty
street of boxes to a glen, a labyrinth where dazed couples
 maundering home of nights could lose their way
a minute from their doors.

Extract reproduced from *Fire-Stick Farming: Selected Poems 1972–90*
(Hale & Iremonger, 1990)

THE BRIDE OF BYFIELD

Jena Woodhouse (b.1949)

The bride is marrying flamboyants:
see her standing where their limbs
brand her dress with fiery tokens,
nimbus her with crimson fronds.

She is marrying dense forest —
pines that make her drunk with resins,
touching her in dreams
with passions whispered and forgone.

At her elbows in attendance
slender pink grevilleas
offer soft vignettes of feathers —
dark green pigeons; finches; doves.

The bride of Byfield is in love
with angels incarnate as trees,
their great wings shedding
crimson petals, resins, and cicada song.

Reproduced from *Eros in Landscape*
(Jacaranda Press, 1989)

Ellis Rowan (1848–1922)
[Grevillea robusta Cunningham, Queensland] 1880s
gouache and watercolour on paper; 55 x 38 cm
Pictorial Collection R2217

REMEMBER?

৯

Eva Johnson

Born by river
Gently rested on a lily pad
Woman—tired eyes
Wading beside filling string bag with lily roots,
     fish, small tortoise, buds
Woman—singing

Around fire, night time sitting
With Kin—sharing food
        cooked in hot ashes
Children laughing,
       Mother singing
   baby on breast
Women telling stories, sharing, giving
Songs, spirit names, teaching
    IN LANGUAGE

No more river—Big dam now
String bag empty
      Supermarket now
Women sitting in big houses
         sharing, singing, remembering
   Mother crying, baby clinging
Women telling stories,
     new stories, new names
        NEW LANGUAGE …

Reproduced from *Inside Black Australia*
(Penguin, 1988)

Ellis Rowan (1848–1922)
Nympaea [i.e. Nymphaea] sp. c.1886
gouache and watercolour on paper; 56 x 38 cm
Pictorial Collection R2087

ACKNOWLEDGEMENTS

ঽ

The National Library of Australia wishes to thank the following for giving their permission to publish poems in this book:

Jena Woodhouse: her poem 'The Bride of Byfield'
HarperCollins Publishers: Extract from Ethel Anderson's 'Eve of Sunday'; extract from James McAuley's 'Canticle'; David Campbell's 'Orchid and Blackboy'
Lee Riley: Extract from Harold Stewart's '30 Haiku'
Jane Diplock: Roland Robinson's extract from 'Tumult of the Swans'
ETT Imprint: Judith Wright's 'Wonga Vine'
ETT Imprint and Paul Slessor: Kenneth Slessor's 'South Country'
Meg Stewart: Douglas Stewart's 'Domestic Poem'
Penguin Australia: Eva Johnson's 'Remember?'
Timoshenko Aslanides: his poem 'Sturt's Desert Pea, *Swainsona formosa*'
Mark O'Connor: an extract from his poem 'Planting the Dunk Botanic Gardens'